It is a Tip!

by Tim Little
Illustrated by Bill Ledger

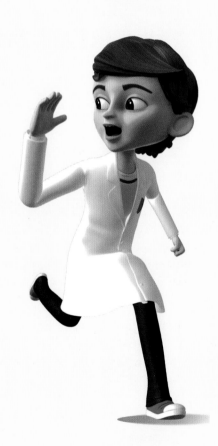

OXFORD
UNIVERSITY PRESS

In this story ...

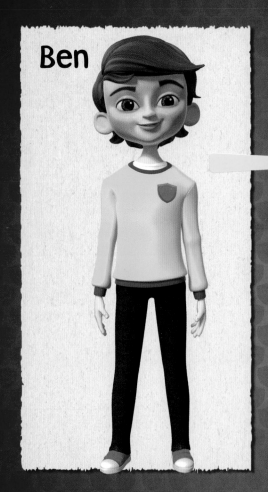

Ben

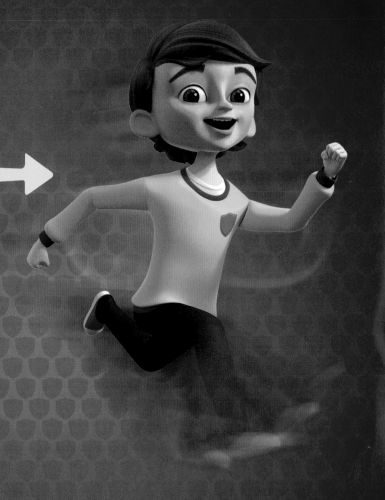

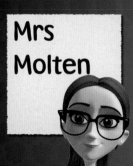

Mrs Molten

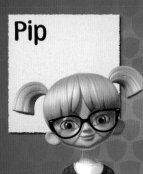

Pip

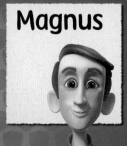

Magnus

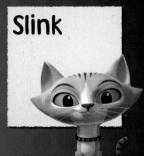

Slink

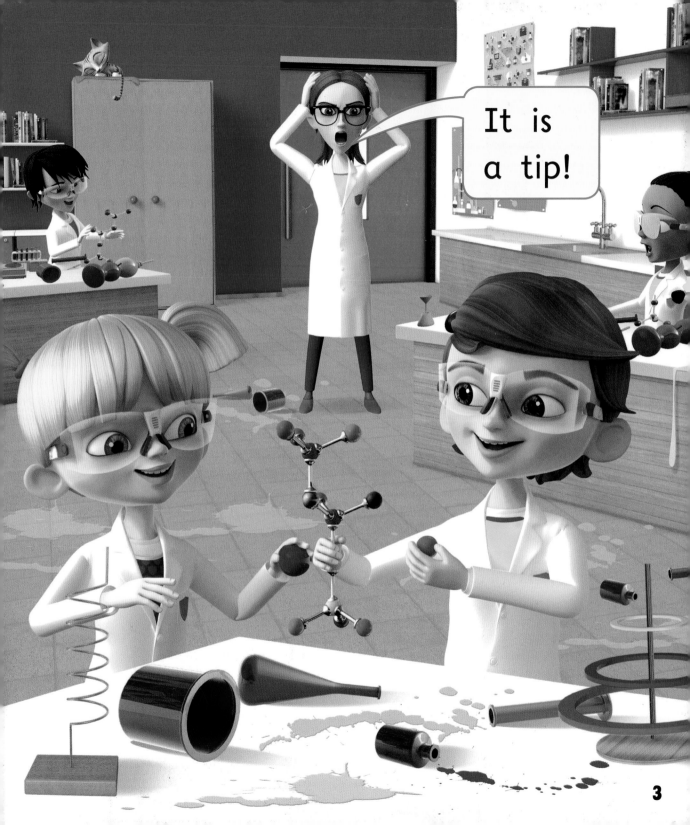

It is
a tip!

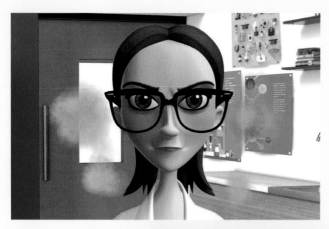

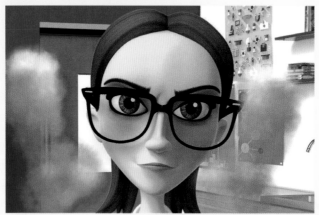

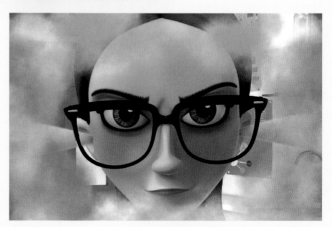

Mrs Molten is mad.

4

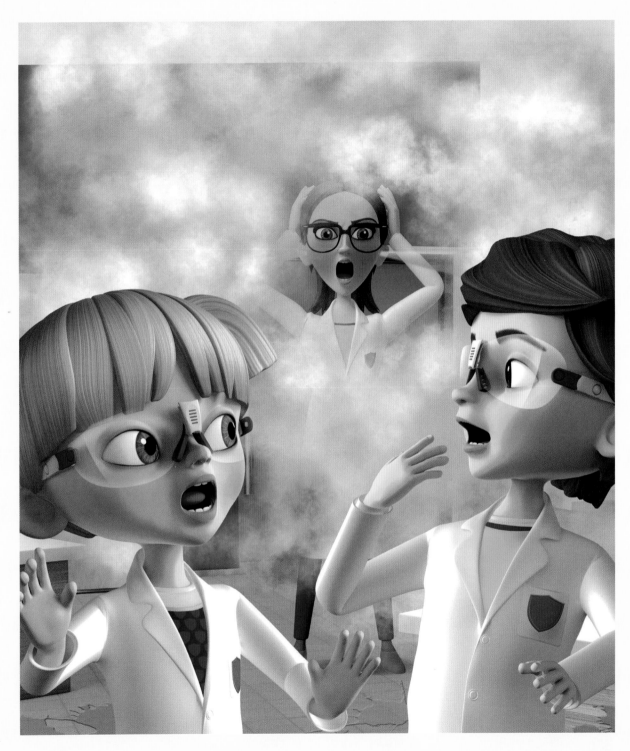

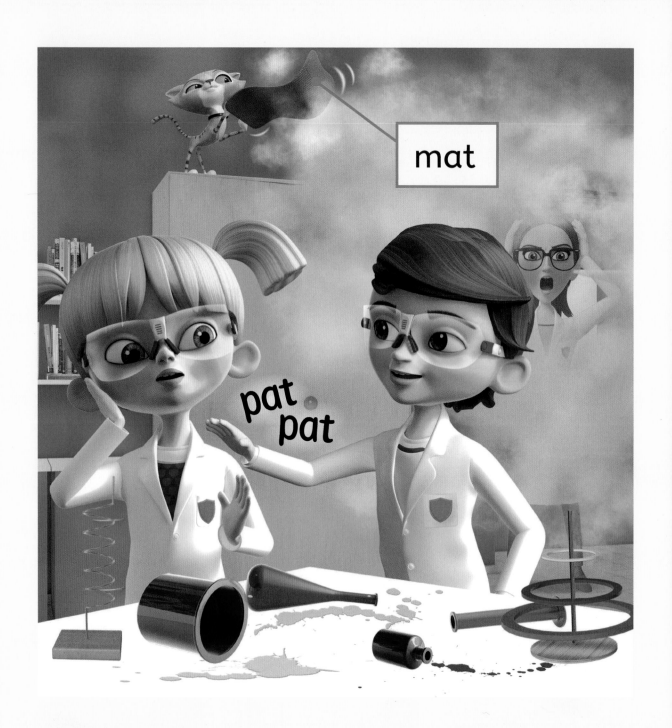

Pip is sad.

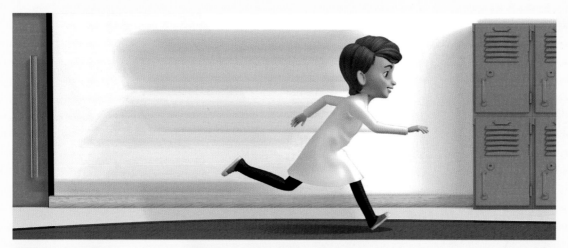

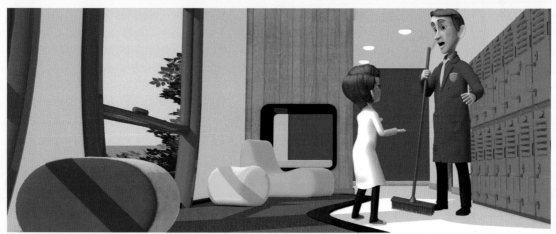

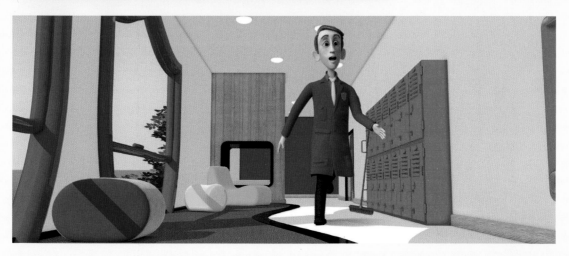

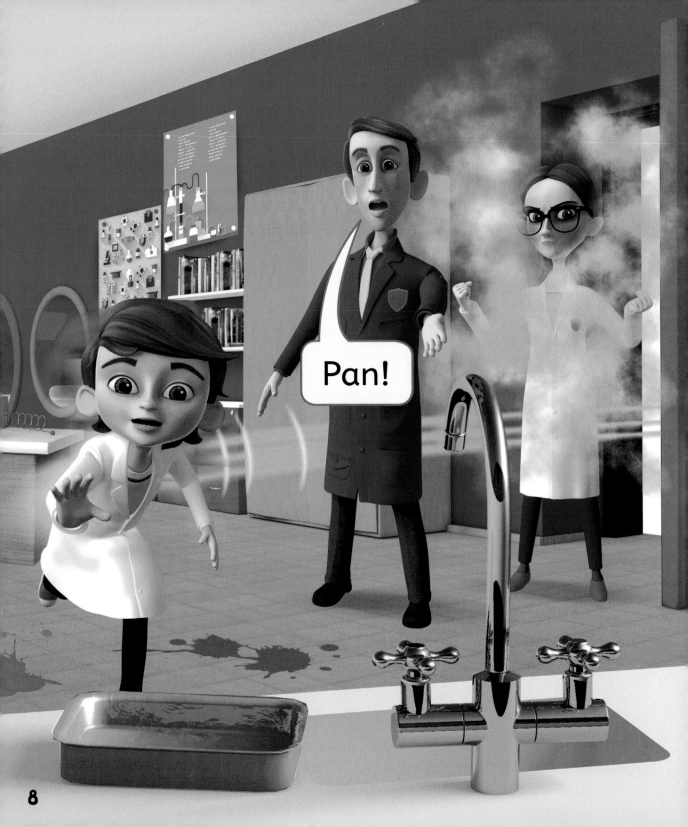

8

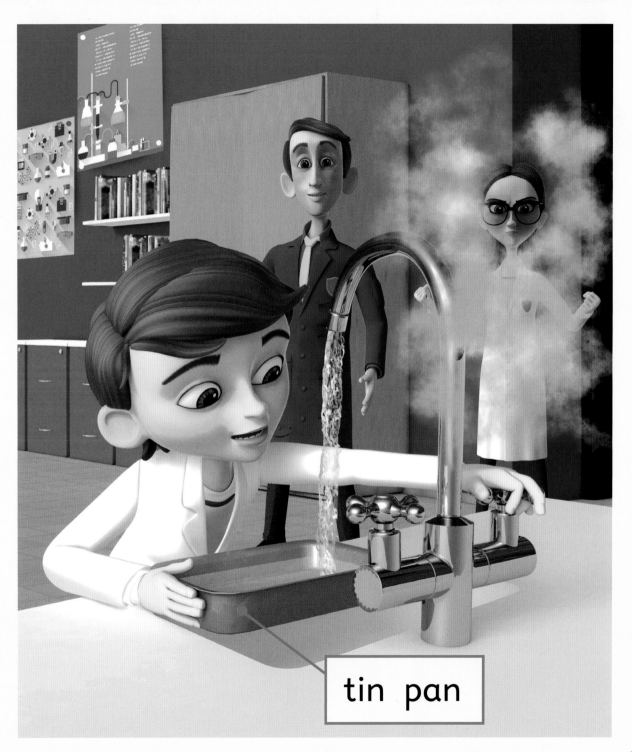

tin pan

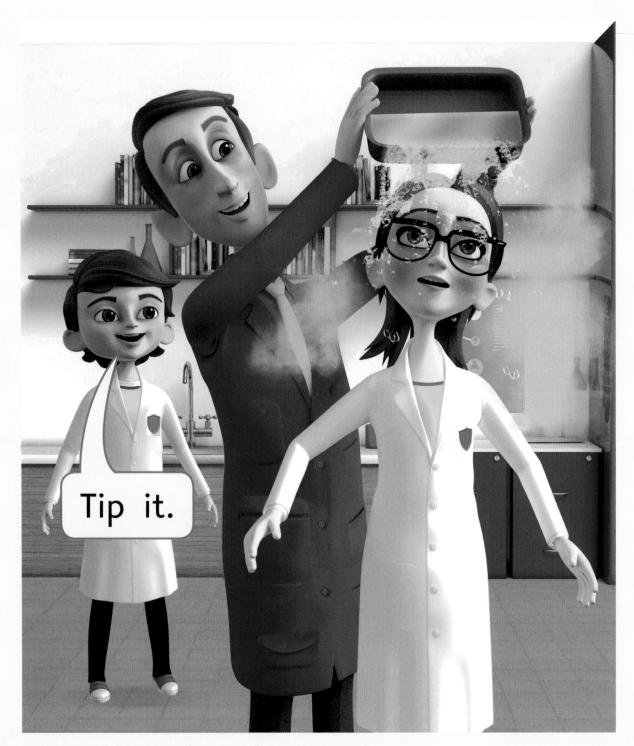

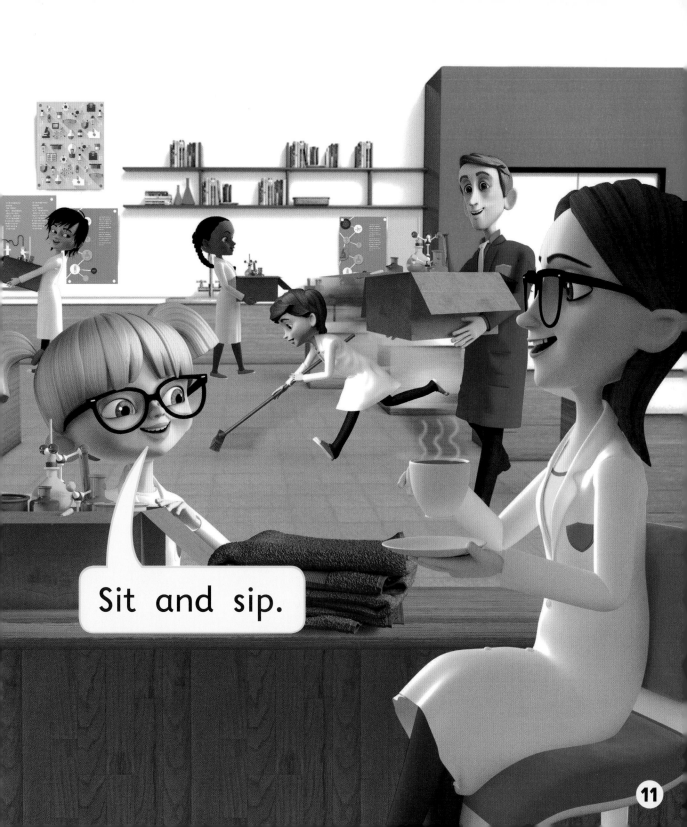

Retell the story ...

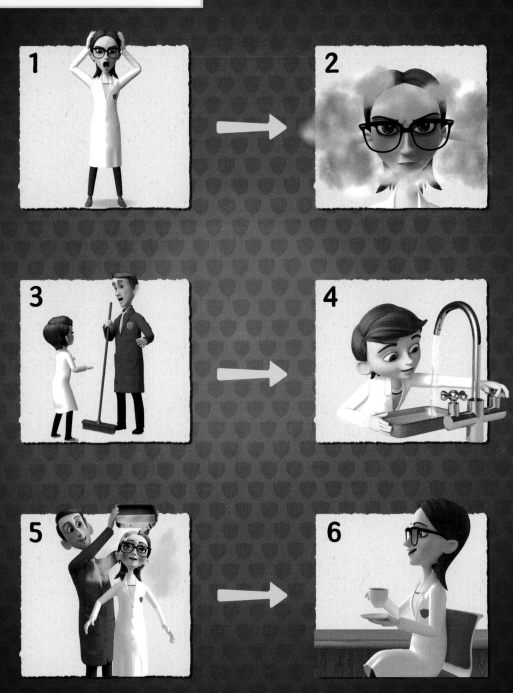